STRANGER
ON A STRANGE PLANET

JEREMY BELL

Caliburn

First Published 1999 by
Caliburn
133a Irsha Street
Appledore
Devon, EX39 1RY

isbn 1 -898546 -36 -3

STRANGER ON A STRANGE PLANET

by

JEREMY BELL

By the same author:
The Grail Prophecy
1996
(available from Caliburn)

Typeset Printed and Bound by
Edward Gaskell
Lazarus Press
Unit 7 Caddsdown Business Park
Bideford Devon EX39 3DX

Dedicated to
all of us who know we know so little—
and still care

Shut the doors, stoke up the fire
And listen to the musings of this poet,
The language of dreams:
You who have little time to ponder
Listen to a heart that beats
Out a rhythm of love
Enmeshed in fears and hopes
Proclaiming truths
In all their savage beauty.

Contents

Part 1: **Environment**

Part 2: **Faith**

Contents

Part 2: **Faith** (continued)

Part 3: **People and Politics**

FOREWORD

These poems were written over a period of three years between 1995-98. Together, they form a very varied collection both in terms of style and content.

Few people, I suspect read a book of poetry from cover to cover. They dip into it, and then if their interest is captured, dip in again. As a general help towards this I have divided the poems into three sections to provide some sort of rough guide as to their content.

Some are very personal — emotional responses to my own experiences and those that friends have shared with me. Others deal with my own ongoing journey 'out of Plato's Cave' — from the psychological games of politics and religion towards the reality of individual faith. The rest are more objective and satirical — snap-shots of 'bureaucratic metro-man'.

If I had to stand back and select a principal underlying theme it would be that of anger at the destructive effects of fundamentalism and of mass consumer culture on the growth of the individual and the global eco-system.

It is my hope that all the poems are 'accessible' (a much maligned word in some literary quarters). Some may shock, some inspire and some provoke, but if any strike responsive chords in those that read them I shall have achieved my objective.

Part 1:
Environment

'HOMO-IGNORAMUS'

The animals held a summit
Linked telepathically,
A crisis meeting to discuss
'Humankind—the Enemy'.
Beneath an old acacia tree
Chairman lion gave a growl;
'Homo-ignoramus' rule
Threatens every fish and fowl,
Free-ranging and farmed quadrupeds
And the poor of their own kind;
There are three options I can see
To cure man's ravening mind.
We could unite and kill them all
And betray their misplaced trust;
Pretend we're all as mad as them
Help them turn the earth to dust;
Or a tenth of every species
Could select an awesome day
And fearlessly destroy themselves—
It's just possible they may
Wake up, take stock of what they've done
And repent their stupid pride
And come and make their peace with us
For the sake of those who died.'
His low growl ceased, he sniffed the wind
Reading his listener's mind- then
Heard the caw of a wise jackdaw—
'I'm not sure I can find
Too much logic in these options,
But I think there is a fourth—

The most exploitive of humanity
Seem to all live in the North.
I suggest a mass migration
To the Southern Hemisphere,
Let the poor and starving eat us,
Show we animals still care.
The silent skies and empty fields
Will reveal our sacrifice;
The survival of creation
May be worth this heavy price'

A dread quiet filled the telesphere
As each animal took stock
Of their terrible position
Twixt a hard place and rock.
But then upon the solemn air
Was heard the strangest ringing,
Massed choirs of bacteria
And viruses were singing.
'A billion, billion of us bugs
Live on every human's skin,
Inside his every orifice,
We're his nearest kith and kin.
We, the lowliest life of all
Have no enemy or friend,
Yet, we the lords of man's proud life,
Have already planned his end.
His sterile purposes are vain
Before our mutating power,
The more unnatural he becomes
Quicker draws his dying hour'.

And this is why all creatures stare
At homo-ignoramus;
The rabid ruler of the earth
Is fatally contagious

BABEL 2 — AND AFTER

Sterile Seeds of Information
Burst from out a billion pods
Seeth around the still-heart centre
Meeting place of men and gods

Congeal upon the still eye-centre
Form cataracts of soulless white—
The fertile earth is disappearing
Disk-bit encoded — lost to sight

Pure instruments of nature's music
Stringed-wind in woodland, chanting seas
Choralling birds and whispering winds
Noised out by alien frequencies

More frenzied groes the work on Babel
That ancient sef-defining dream
Where man may meet himself in god-head—
A flea bestriding nature's stream

Web-wired, mouse-mazed in virtual space
An ant-heap empire out of time
From birth to death conscripting all
One global mass-production line

Selecting only useful life-forms
Processing them with crushing care
The re-gened superman emerges
Defiant in his desert-bare

Of nature's differentiation
Of every snowflake, fish and bird
Each plant, each animal — each human's
Unique emotion, spoken word

—'Til spirit's madness, shaping symbol
Deep culverted beneath the earth
Erupts — and pours its molten meanings
In elemental, manic-mirth

Along the lignified lost lifeways
Spring-rampant, vagrant, gushing red
Short-circuiting the picture shadows
On cave walls of the living dead

Bud-tender—healing life-floods open
Deaf spirit ears — long blinded eyes
And human throats so long constricted
Sing out new star-songs through the skies

§

FOR THE LOVE OF BRITAIN

Here in the lucky Western Isles
The dreams of the world have been sown,
Seeds from the sacred Tree of Life
Lie asleep in her hills of stone;
Planted here by the Sons of God
Till the star-dew draws the sting, and
The Wasteland stirs and springs to life
At the call of the Fisher-King

An alchemy of healing herbs
Grew rich and thick in field and wood
And breathed deep magic through the air
Which men inspired and understood,
And wove within their crystal dreams
A spirit of benevolence
Transcendent, yet so wondrous close,
Gnosis of deep omnipresence.
Tuned to their heartland's beating pulse
This vision like a violet grew -
A scent of heaven that winter's blight
Could never quench — but spring anew
In every wakened native heart,
A harmony of earth and soul
Resonating through the kingdom
Where God and man could each extol,
Communing with each variant life,
Animal, insect, bird and child,
Tending the freedoms each declared
Lightly touching the rampant wild.

And lately, there were rolling downs,
The lark's song and the bumble bee,
Bluebell woods and hedgerows ripe
With fruit and flower and shading tree,
And badger sets in mossy banks
And fieldmice in the waving corn,
And tendril paths among the crops
And rivers where the salmon spawned.
These kept within the English mind
A spirit of the wondering kind.

The downs are rent with concrete gulfs
For fetid streams of cursing cars,
A lark lies bleeding by a cone
And dying — whispers to the stars.
Straight, crew-cut hedges sullen stand
Barren of fruit and flower and nest
Guarding the mono-cultured crops
Last refuges for bug and pest.
Ecologists record the wake,
And murmer to the friends of earth
While Priests of Progress wring their hands
And rape the land that gave them birth
This is the England we have made
This is the land that we've betrayed.

The ghosts of England's heroes watch,
Brooding on the slopes of Badon
The omnipresent cameras
Form the firing squads of freedom,
And numbers fall like freezing hail
Clamping the land with iron fist —
The spirit's glory hovering
Then — reluctantly withdrawing,
Grieving — behind the holy mist.

'Tell me the worth of an English wood,
The cost of a nightingale's song,
The market price of eagle's eggs,
Whether owls and badgers belong
Anymore in your tidy, paved park
Where your withering hand holds sway,
And freedom's wind and freedom's sky
Are straining their shackles each day?'

Silent, pass the forced migrations,
Transplanted, herded from their land
By the masters of production
To reservations of the damned;
Round the fringes of the cities,
Fenced, concentrated in green camps,
A baggage — heritage of dreams
Remembered on New Issue Stamps.
This is the England we have made
These are the lives that we've betrayed.

Smell the raging funeral pyres,
Gas-ovens built for slaughtered cows,
The prison camps of battery hens
And dark, veal pens and crated sows
This is the England we have made
These are the lives that we've betrayed.

Re-fashion more productive genes,
Cloned lamb and shocked self-shearing ewe
New, fatless pigs and steers and hens -
Stay dumb — and sup this devil's brew.
This is the England we have made
These are the lives that we've betrayed.

The heavens rend, and angry light
Stunts feeble growth, and burns the skin.
No barrier cream can shield the truth
Or salve a traitor's cancered sin.
This is the England we have made
Ours is the life that we've betrayed.

'Tis Power, Power — the great delusion;
Shall man leave sucking nature's breast,
Plot a path of evolution,
Build an inorganic nest, where
He's the sole imperial master
Constructing empires in the stars?
You fools — those burnt out bunkers scream
Behold — the frenzied power of Mars!'

Be still, be still — take off your shoes,
See — the sacred land is burning'
Her children's eyes are filled with soot,
And their hearts cry out for healing.

Does Earth need blood to give her life,
And bone ground down before she'll yield?
No. She offers each her daily bread
If they but join her in the field.

Life to the land — our souls inter
Deep underground in Avalon
Till ancient visions break their bonds
And germinate in Albion.

§

THE END OF NATURE

The dark is no longer natural
Sodium lights now taunt the stars
Starving it of mystery.

The daylight is no longer natural
We have rent the heavens
And the sun glares at us.

The sky is no longer natural
Sunsets are glazed with chemical colourings
Smoldering in the burnished blue.

The wind is no longer natural
It blows from man-made deserts,
Burning forests and concrete cities
The dust and dioxides of human excrement.

The rain is no longer natural
Diluted with additives,
It is now powerless
To baptise my daughter's hair.

The rivers and streams are no longer natural
They are sterile clear
Running like athletes on steroids.

The subtle symphony of nature can no longer be heard
Except in snatches — in desert places
The tinitis of traffic drowns the choral of the lark.

*My children will never find that space
That unmapped, pristine place
Of the untrammeled wild
Where I walked as a child.*

APOCALYPSE

The darkening stage is milling full
Of actors groping for a script,
A Babel internet of bytes
Chatters around the global crypt.

Telephones ring, a choir sings as
The last thrush croaks its lullaby.
Love-embers smoulder in the gloom,
Fire-bursts of lust explode and die.

Armies of steel and leathered gangs
Parade beneath their tribal flags;
Pinched shoppers scurry through the malls
With sterile food in groaning bags.

Image clad, each entombed spirit
Wrestles with communication,
Calculates each withered word,
Costs the impact of creation.

Vain wait for each new wintered spring
For fresh blood-rush to penile stem,
But a sunbeam, lost, dust-dancing
Tickles the hopes of scratching men.

§

OF VANITY AND VISION

The precious pains, the sceptic pains,
The lying light of fractured stars,
The dying dreams that lose their names,
That mock, as innocence expires.

Sunk deep beneath their awful weight,
Museumed within the calloused earth,
Yet tender still — they mourn their fate
And lie about their tarnished worth.

A tinselled fir — bright, fairy-lit,
Red crêpe around its rootless trunk;
A day's hope, void of infinite,
And sterile as a cloistered monk.

And then I saw a seedling sprout,
Painfully from the bloody sod,
Faith-watered in the human drought,
And flowering, bear the fruit of God.

§

REFLECTIONS

If the sun clouded her face, withdrew her life-light
From her only fertile child and its mad keepers
Embarrassed by the staring stars:
If the rain came cautiously, grey-trickling,
An old dog watering his last lamppost
Running dry:
If the Arctic easterly blew and blew,
Chill-creeping through cotton dresses,
Numbing the Spring:
If the frost descended on the branch,

Bone-crunching its needle way
Into the marrow:-
Acid-dripping, cold-cramping, soul-splintering;
Then men would still fight
Cross-cursing, faithfully fearing
Their little deaths.

* * *

Take the joy of heaven
And bury it deep in human clay
Such that it flames the heart
And sparks the limbs.
Let war and pestilence ravage it
'Til it screams for release,
Or with proud, stoic dignity
Sacrificially endures;
Or nurturing the love-seeds
Waits and watches

Light-feeding, stem-reaching,
Bud-opening
Into too early blossom
Blasted by the hail of human winter.

§

THE PROPHESYING WIND

Will you not listen
To the hysterical wind,
The unchained, rebel lunatic
Screaming the agonies
Of the dumb
Cowering in the chainsawed wilderness,

Galeing at the suicidal empire
Of tarmac and concrete
That drips its alien compounds
Into the aquifers
Of the struggling earth?
She smells of the stinking skins of beasts,
Locusts and mosquitos are her portents
For the white, sterilised suckers
Videoing there lives away
In self-locking cages,
Climatically controlled,
Filtering there own pollution
And untamed fears.

Burn, burn the goddess Gai;
Though her wild innards
Are but half understood

Even when dissected;
Reconstitute her genes
In your own defaced image.
For your feet —
Too sensitive for suffering
But cruel enough to trample
Become leprous
Stumbling over her prostrate carcass
As you —
Lust mournfully over the kill,
This death — your death
Of untried lives,
This death that need not be.

§

THE HUMBLING

In dreams, I saw the star-dark gathering
Conspiring with the sun's cohorts,
'Terra's tyrants wound our pleasure,
Free her elemental demons and
Dissolve their reason with our sports'.

I heard a half-grown vandal wind
Plotting with a vagrant sea
Tempted by a maddening moon,
'Outlaw rebels we shall be.
I will fetch the knuckled hailstones
That love to fight with flail and stud
Bring them from their winter wasteland
To our feast of human blood:

So, heap up the tides upon their shores
Deluge the land with water,
Engulf their streets with rock and mud
And smash their bricks and mortar.
Splinter the air with thunderbolts
Whip them from their bunkered beds
Strike with searing spears of lightning
Fling their tiles upon their heads.
Though some may curse and some may pray
We fear neither good not evil
Loosed are we barbaric angels
Agents both of God and Devil.'

§

REALITY

Adzed timbers, chiselled stones and thatch,
Built in the knowledge that man must watch
The forest creeping round the tower,
The frost upon the wilting flower.
Nature is but combed and brushed.

The lichened grave stones lean and fall
Down the well of memory,
And ruined Babels testify
'Build your towers and idols high,
Knowing well that each must die;
Whatever dream that comes to pass
Must one day sleep beneath the grass'

§

THWARTED DREAMS

A scoffing wind, a mocking wind
Spitting at the swirling dreams
Sly — seeping from the praying roofs
Clustering round the siren beams
Sparkling in the sodium light
Mooning by the factory wall
The prison of the rigid day —
Absorbed within their concrete shawl —
Hear them whispering away
In deep catacombs of longing
Behind doors of no — more — pain,
They're conspiring and they're scheming
And tonight, they'll rise again.

§

'PROGRESS'

'There is no alternative',
You can't halt progress —
Else we'd all go to sleep
Beneath all that waiting greenery
— Like our ancestors.'

My car is as big as my image
And cost thirty grand.
It can go thirty times as fast
As a jogger
And keep going —
Though most of the time
I crawl along
Belted in gridlock
Fuming in greenbelt
Behind tinted windows.
Protected by steel bumper bars
I can hit a fat pheasant,
Pretend it's a gawping peasant,
Or the occasional badger or cat —
You don't have to stop for that-
On my way down
From my first home
To my second
For two weeks a year.

It's good to relax amongst
Slow, uninteresting people.
When I retire, I'll join CPRE
And fight to protect it all.

ANGER OF ONE-DIMENSIONAL MAN

Would that I could shoot a swallow
Blast it from the clear blue skies
Oblivious to the tears of heaven
The pain within my children's eyes

Would that I could stab a syringe
In the neck of chimpanzee
Content that science and religion
Will justify my infamy

Would that I could fell a jungle
Create a burger-ranch instead
Make a factory of farming
Turn creation on its head

Would that I could conquer nature
Systemise its vagrant wild
Patent every gene I find there
Breed the genius super-child

Would that I could be immortal
Be forever twenty-five
Love a hundred thousand women
Drink a vat of '45

Would that I could break this silence
Shatter it with blasting sound
Fill my empty life with riches
Before I'm buried in the ground

§

LAST PETAL

Only the mad — the dumb dreamers
Heard
The last pink petal sigh
On her fragile fluttering
Downward — deadward
Even they
Did not see, did not reach,
Try to pluck
The wounded flower
From my thornless stem;
Take my sacrifice
And press its fading colour warmth
Against another's breast'

This maimed mutation,
Irradiated — too weak to grasp?
Is become a useless weakling
In a beeless world.
Better the roar of neutered power,
The mega-tonnage,
The megabytes,
The sterile concrete —
Than the prophetic silence,
The softening pain
Of a falling petal.

§

QUESTIONS I CANNOT ANSWER

"Tell me the time; please tell me the time,"
Soft-questioned my own trusting child.
"How long will the Earth swing round the sun
Before there're no lions in the wild?

Will the ozone layer disappear?
Will the plants all wither and die?
Will we be able to sledge again
As the Earth gets hotter and dry?

Will I see playful dolphins and whales,
And will there be fish in the sea?
Will there be jungles, when I grow up,
That I will be able to see?

Will elephants, tigers and hippo
Still be roaming the lands they knew?
Or will they be fenced in like prisoners,
Look as sad as those in the zoo?

Will there be streets where I can still play
Safely without being molested?
You've watched TV; will you play with me
In the garden, now you've rested?"

I didn't reply, but got to my feet,
No excuses, I'm on the 'dole'.
And I knew as his small hand clasped mine,
It was me he tried to console.

§

AUTUMN

Come the cold, reforming gales,
Iconoclasts of life's profusion
To gust at summer's luxury
Tear down her coloured canopy —
She cringes, crying-wet
Bare faced beneath accusing skies,
Pleading, penitential
Stiffening, puritanical
Hid in long, black-hooded nights
And white, nail-bitten days.

The organ plays her requiem
Asthmatic through the creaking tree-lofts;
Lit our easy living's bonfires
Curling, swirling incense round
The crinkled congregation of leaves
Rustle-whispering impatiently
Amongst brittle amputated limbs
Waiting for the white service to begin.

Bold as a blackmailer steals Halloween
Magot-wriggling into wrinkled apples
Worm-pulling muck and stubble down
Down into the hibernating underworld,
While oozing, fly-blown berry drops
Imprisoned nuts and bitter-late sloes
Hang on — heavy with cold
Hovering like late mourners
Around summer's grave.

§

THE GREAT DIVORCE

'You shall be as gods, knowing good from evil'
(The serpent)

Recognising no higher court,
We announce our divorce
From this untamed woman,
(On the grounds of unreasonable behaviour)
She has exposed us to the staring stars
And made us feel small and naked;

Therefore, we will clothe ourselves — independently,
And tame her wild jungles and oceans.
Does she think we are mere men — primitives
Obliged to live with her idiosyncratic moods?
We are gods—
And will use her for our own gratification
While we build a new home for ourselves.

§

BUTTERFLY GREENS

Playing with his jigsaw of genes,
Computerising memories;
Self-numbered, economically ordered,
Dressed and aerosoled by the market —
No mess, no sweat,
Safe sex with flavoured condoms for safe men —
'Just a quickie then
Or we'll miss the mummer play'

'There's money in recycling traditions,
Sifting the detritus for vestiges of the spirit;
We could put our community on the map —
Re-enact mock battles and burnings —
But we'd have to market it well.
Did you know that Ilfracombe's Victorian Festival
Attracted 1/4 million visitor nights last year?
We could do the same — it's so quiet here.
That's what people come for — to get away from it all.
But we'd have to upgrade the road,
We could have a visitor centre,

And sell good, wholesome food;
Not those dirty mis-shapes of fruit and veg
Or the regularised, refined, cellophaned
Supermarket products —
But something in between —
Organic perhaps?
And Morris Men — so vigorous and virile,
Makes my sperm count rise —
I got that NHS operations video out,
Do you want to see it?'

SEA LOVER — PART 1

I sing her love's fresh freedom;
Her running tides flow in my blood.
Diving into her deep nakedness
She covers what I'd leave behind;
Walking reluctantly away from her
She exposes the shores of my dreams
Waiting my return
To soak playfully in her mystery;
And then, ever attentive
She'll lap and suck and caress,
Or with sudden, urgent outpouring
Sweep me up, bidding me ride
The white wildness of her passion
Until exhausted, I fall again
Into the sweet smoothness of her slumber.
I even love her grey depressions
When she withdraws behind an autumn fog
Reaching sombrely out to me, lapping my feet
With her great black tongue.
Many times, with heavy heart have I left her
'I will come back' Silently, she blew
Salt kisses at my back and waved.

Along the metalled, ribbed-roadways,
(Had she lived here once?)
I drove over nature
To the city of the deaf
Where the tinnitis of machines
Jerk the chains of men.
Like a faithless lover, I peddled my soul
For a mess of mortgage-and cried.

When it was done, my body dulled,
My spirit numb with noise,
I came back — to her warm waiting,
And she — she brought me her crafted wood
Laying it neatly on the shore.
'I knew you would come back to me;
I have made these for you'.
I looked at her — January's steel fingers
Raping the warmth from my clothes.
In my cottage, I laid her gifts upon my grate
And sacrificed them with her brother Fire,
Watching her body-salt seeping and hissing,
Genie — swirling from the golden caverns,
Ghosting up through the dark funnel,
While I sat bathed in her gift-warmth
Listening to her siren songs
Washing the wounded night.

§

SEA LOVER — PART 2

Then she blew —
Furiously — scorning my calm reasoning;
Because of my reasonableness.
I could read the signs,
Feel the swell rising,
The sullen power beneath her oily calm
That betrayed her frustration.
I rode her — reefing my mainsail,
But when she began to break,
Washing over my calm pleadings
Spitting in my face,
I took it down
Relying only on naked gib,
The cutting edge of intuition
To steer over
Her confused passion.

But she blew — I knew she would;
She had to get it out of her system,
To hurt me into loving
Her deep vulnerability.
I made the mistake of laughing in her face,
Fear — excitement?
I had nothing to lose but her:
She could swallow me
And weep salt later.
We shouted at each other,
We screamed,
She threw herself at me,
Hating my frailty.
"I love your madness
As much as I fear it.

I cannot conquer you —
Do not want to;
But I will not drown in you.
How can I hate my mother,
My mistress — my lover,
My friend of my lone-dream
You who bear me toward my horizon".
And then I wasn't laughing —
I was bailing furiously,
Angrily — fearfully — desperately.

"Though you win, I still love you."
And then, noticeably — suddenly
A lull — was she answering
I heard her groan — her wet fists
Hammering more half- heartedly,
— willing me
To cream through her rhythmic waves.

Raising my mainsail again,
Pounding urgently through her,
I assured her of our meeting.
And when later — exhausted, I slept
Upon the regular swell of her soft crests,
My heart beating against hers,
I felt her kiss my wanting
As she bore me onwards.

§

RAIDER

In the blackout
I watched
Breakers of cloud
Tearing at an anchored moon,
While below
A blackened sea,
Stealthy as a commando
Raided the shore
Retreating
Unobserved.
A plane growled once
But didn't see.
As the dark burnt away
I saw
Scavenging seagulls,
Eight wingless fishing boats
Grounded in the mud
And one gaunt, long — limbed man,
Gum — booted and bandy — legged
Scuttling
Toward them.

Part II:
Faith

DANCING MYTHS

Only the weighting granite,
Frozen energy,
Seasoned by time to grotto-space,
Unused entrance to the
infin
ite.
In the hallowed hour
Of melting sunrise
A pilgrim —
Standing transfixed
Between anxiety and hope,
Faith-fused to a marble Virgin.
'Madonna, my closet mother,
Whose shining Son can capture
The almighty power of distant fatherhood,
Give me a sign.'

Unconsciously,
The spirit's searching template
Gently shakes,
Shapes
The resonating quantum,
And time dissolves,
Unfreezing holy matter.
She moves!
The Virgin moves a benedictional limb
And oozes tears
From out a thawing duct
Baptising the aching dream
With time's confusion.

Before the sun had frowned again
Three hundred others streamed
Towards this gate in Heaven,
Waiting—willing its reopening;
And early next day
A casuistic priest,
Self-crucified upon the crossbar
Of eternal hope and temporal power,
Does not enter in — but
Listens patiently
Before reporting to his Bishop;
And he, neither blessing nor condemning,
Waits,
Carefully appraising
The popularity
Of this new persuasion.
(In dreams, he wonders why
He and his flock should rarely see
Such visions in the mass
So vividly,
Rather than in a bare rock shrine
Outside
In the untamed
Weathered wilderness.)

And there — a fruit, casually sliced
Reveals in sacred writ
The Name of the Prophet.
And there — a sacred cow
With plaster teats
Gives milky signs
For the semi-blind.

And there — heavenly rain
Dripping through a subway roof
Paints the Virgin on a pavement,
Provides for some a living proof —
For the bruised and burdened,
Thirsty for the ambrosia,
The affirming exudence
From out eternity,
Aghast at the global autopsy and
Proliferation of numbered parts,
The self-fracturing analysis.

Yet, still the sacred softly seeps
Through the perforated planet,
Oily
Between the clamouring, grinding cogs
That crush the living
Beneath its overarching wheel;
And still, arthritically,
Self consciously,
The prayer beads thumb
Their dumb beseechings
To the Prince of Spheres.
'Teach us the long forgotten songs,
The dance steps
Your exiled earth,
Sunk in amnesia
No longer plays.'

§

DEVIL AND MUSTARD SEED

Down in the dark,
The deep heart-dark
In a black hole
Of implacable silence
The blind numen sucks
The unconscious noosphere,
Telepathically transmitting
Drip by acid drip
His parasitic demons
Of guilt and fear
Into the flickering light.

A woman—
Shrouding her flickering hope,
Shrouded for shame
Outcast — haemorrhaging
With the blood men fear
Presses through a stubbled crowd —
Reaches between stiff, moral backs
And dares the lightest touch:
A septic finger dips into a clear spring,
A spark of faith leaps over a synapse
Of uncertainty
Towards a robe
Impregnated with love.
He stops and turns.
'Who touched me?'
'In all this jostling throng?'
'Someone touched me;
Power has gone out from me'
(The numen stirs and spits
Agitating the life-repressing men)

They search around
Lusting to accuse
Condemn — stone.
Trembling, she stumbles forward
Dragging herself through the clashing shadows
Towards the love-creating light.
They shrink back,
Hissing between spittled teeth
'Despicable — impure
Infectious, aged ewe'
The Word sounds — resonates
'You are accepted,
Go in peace,
Your faith has healed you.'

§

DANCE

There is no retreat.
Alive—we must dance
Upon the stage
Until our part is ended.

We were not born as sentries,
As guards against uncertainty,
Self-made excrusions
Of space and time's strange tracery,
Painted backdrops for an unscripted epic,
Bitter-humble props
Poulticing the soul,

Seeking to draw the acid loneness
From bandaged hearts;
Sublimating the fearful tension,
Weaving it into rituals,
Making sacrifices of non-participation
To our onerous gods;
Life's taut thread trembling
In the mocking breeze
Of others swirling movement.
Opiate and alcohol
Dampen the nerve and fire the brain,
Mercenaries retained
To fight the demon army,
Till paid a higher price,
Change sides
And open up the gates.

Cry out now — and wait:
The spirit on the trackless stage
Blows moist upon the wizened seed
Inside its oaken image,
And softening calls the sleeping soul
To rise and laugh
And leap to life
And follow dancing in its wake.

§

PLATO'S CAVE

Mimed shadows on the cavern walls,
Dancing dimly, flickering warmly,
Reflected choreography,
The ebb and flow of known emotions,
The oiled waves of needy oceans,
Mysteriously acceptable
Life-size, sweetly manageable:
Who dares to shatter these mirrored halls?

Depression sucks at certainty,
Cold, the untouchable centre cries,
Wincing, the phantoms leap with lies,
A bitter storm of cursing demons,
The thwarted power of sleeping shamans:
'They're yours; you moved, my dreams are spurned.
Why? For what? Your soul has turned
To face the fiery forms of beauty'.

§

SCREENPLAY

Plato was right;
The filtered light
Projected onto our silver screens
Reveals the drama and emotions
Of all our dreams.
Sitting tight,
We watch — never rash
Those who get excited —
Orgasmic, by a crash;
Brave explorers,

Our dreams are not so wet —
At least, not yet.
Rape and killing
Each programmed night,
So vicariously thrilling,
Generates just a breath of heat
But little light.
Would the real blood and sweat,
The fear of actual fight
Engaging us
In some hard street
Not painfully mock
Our curious shock?
But never mind.
Autistic, we gaze —
Remotely controlled,
Shadow sailors
Riding out storms
In dock.
Titillated,
Our bunkered brains
Are sworn
To anchor the soul,
Lest it sets its sails,
Makes free voyage
Toward the grails
Of sunrise.
Repressing faith and guilt
We nod — so wordly wise,
Critics of our own destiny,
Masturbators of memory,
Observing the world wilt
And fade before our eyes.

THE LIBERATION OF FOOLS

The prison doors stand open

All the maps where false
Drawn up by crude men
Who travelled in dreams
Towards myths;
Insecure, technically illiterate
They appeased the unknown
Filling the empty spaces
With dragons.
They don't exist — we know that
They all live in here.

The prison doors stand open

We'll follow our own maps —
Intellectually
Every space crammed
With hard facts.
So why go beyond the doors?
Words are safer than action
Evoking pictures,
Memories of feeling
Without risk
Of the foolery
Of chasing meanings
We have analysed away.

The prison doors stand open

The aching vacuum sucks
The wild cyclone
Towards our bunkered spirits.
We wilt before its lash,
Put up the bars
And try and close
The doors again

The prison doors stand open

Some fools are leaving
To test if they are made
Of sentient clay—
And God
And freedom haunts their eyes
And freedom fills their spirits
And freedom grows their souls

The prison doors stand open
Only the fools are saved.

§

REALITIES

Anxiety
Anacondan
Round the guts
Only the sun in the brain
Burns
In the battle-clouds
—Black shrouds
Wound around
Cold courage.

In town,
The night before,
Sex raw
Spurts uninvolved
Inside
A greedy,
Understanding whore
—Helps temper
Self-despising
Agony.

Swarms of metal,
Anonymous
Shred
The shrouds
And skin and bone
—Leave one or two
Un-dead
—Cold-sweating
Shit dribbling,
Crying for the whore—
The last momento
Of the Mother-Lover.

When it was safe
The others came,
The precious mass
Who always watch,
Commentating cleanly,
Casually,
Liberally despising
The messiness
—To record

Photograph
—Tourists
Picking over the remains.

Later,
Re-insured
Gainst scary questions,
Someone made a film
Of disinfected frames,
Like watching
A sanitary towel
Dry—
—For two hours
They re-lived,
Vicariously,
The sterilised
Monstrous agony
Then went their way—
Twittering.

§

FANTASY

'Vulnerable?
Let us embalm your soul.
Your choice —
Distinctive style, flowing lines —
Crimson, black, magenta,
White, emerald or Fijian blue;
Matching, colour-coded bumpers
Creating the sleek appearance,
Concealing the inner strength.
Space and comfort — Air conditioning,

No noise or vibration,
Centrally-locked against
The world out there.

Inside, you are transformed;
Yours is the power
Of sheer drivability.
Your sure footed performance-
Inside your Armani suit,
Your Gucci shoes,
Behind the tinted windows
With panoramic views,
Will leave everyone else behind.
No one will know you.'

When cancer calls,
Divorce divides,
And the sarcophagus splits open
Revealing the preserved image;
When your soft self is left
Exposed upon the verge
Crying at the metal tide
Roaring through its tarmacced gulf,
Dying for its fantasy —
Let it die;
Yours is not the only wreck
Grounded on this concrete coast —
It is littered with
Broken down bangers
Like yourself —
Raw, nude souls
Irrigating hope,
Growing meanings together
In the waiting wilderness.

OF GOD AND GODOT

Dreamers masturbating
Waiting in the park
Terrified of living
Crying in the dark.

Godot won't be coming
Godot doesn't care
Godot's the Ferrari
Seen in Leicester Square.

Godot's the Life-waster
Godot is a clown
Godot's Lottery numbers
Never written down.

Godot's not in Heaven
Godot's not on Earth
Dreams of saviour Godot
Always die at birth.

God is not a Muslim
God is not a Jew
God is not a Buddhist
Nor is he Hindu.

God's not a Catholic
Guarded by a Pope
God's not the Protestant's
Disincarnate hope.

God is not a banker
Weighing the amount
Every living creature
Holds in their account.

God's in dumb animal
God's in chain-sawed tree
God's the tortured captive,
God's the refugee.

God's the urgent lover
Looking for a wife
God's the sacred mother
Nurturing each life.

God is the Barbarian
Never held at bay
Breaking all defences
Standing in his way.

God's the great composer
Living through his dance.
God's the great abetter
Of each taken chance.

Godot's time-bound demon
Pisses on the Earth
God the Holy Spirit
Brings everything to birth.

§

HEAR NO EVIL / SEE NO EVIL

The foetus crying in the womb,
The child locked in a neighbour's room.
The boy abused in early life,
The whimpers of his battered wife.
The silence of the starving man,
The captive in the prison van.
The killings in a foreign land,
The severing of a muslim's hand.
The murder on the silver screen,
The rape of actresses — a dream.
The veal calf in its darkened pen,
The drugged pig and the battery hen.
The fledglings fall — the cat's claw,
The shuddering oak, the screaming saw.
The strangled cry of hound-torn fox,
The quiet rot of AIDS and pox.
The seal cub bludgeoned on the ice,
Experiments on rats and mice.
The perfume tested in the eyes,
And all the other unheard cries
Of life outside the goldfish bowl
Produce a deafness in the soul.

Net cruising through his Babel dream
Men watch their lives pass on a screen

The whole creation groans outside
Waiting the call of groom and bride

CREATING MEANING

How can it really matter
After many billion years
A world explodes in fragments
In a space devoid of prayers,
In a time devoid of meaning
Umpteen light years far away
From us or unknown aliens —
There is nothing you can say
Or do — except to make sure
You're submitted to your fate
And your funeral is paid for
When you reach your sell-by date;
In the meantime, keep working
At your insignificance,
Go boldly to the 'unknown',
Sit every fashion fence;
Avoid deep love and hating
If you'd be respectable
Flap your sails at every wind
Become as forgettable
As a tiny particle
In a shaft of sunlit air —
No-one says it isn't 'dust — right'
They just accept it's there
For a fraction of a moment
They notice it one day
And then get on with worrying
With what the neighbours say,
And whether they are dressed right
Or should drink red wine with meat,
Viagra — the weather
The 'reg.' in the street.

So how to find a meaning
And give substance to your hours,
Though meanings are miasmic
Like smoke from damp bonfires
In space/ time's mad infinite
Consuming the dust of stars
Within unconscious time-spans
Transcending rational powers?

You take the living moment
And laugh within your dreams,
You accept the finite nature
Of your dust within the beams
Of lovelight ever dancing,
And trust there's saving power
Within in this odd creation
After your brief conscious hour;
And face your inner demons
In the shadows of your soul —
There's meaning in your madness,
Your'e not a voodoo doll,
A tormented, stringed puppet
At the mercy of the fates,
You'll be your soul's strong jockey
If you understand your hates
And ride your demons boldly
With integrity and grace;
Use bit and bridle wisely
If you'd find your inner face.

But lift your head in protest
At the meanness of the mind
That counts the cost of loving,
Lives cursing they are blind —
Though always understanding
Why they baulk at every fence,

They dare not — so they win not,
They've little deep faith — sense.
They'll always live life waiting,
They'll keep waiting till they croak
For a fuhrer, a guru
Who'll betray them — go for broke!

Be free to find your meaning,
You have freedom in your will
Though death may haunt your journey
There is meaning in life still
If you except the challenge
Every second, minute hour —
What will you create of this?
Will you live or spurn the power?
Accept — you are transmuted
From your chrysalis of pain
Baulk — become more fossilised,
Harder still to rise again.

There's love beyond your being
If you find the faith to fly
The confines of convention
That define you with a lie
About your spirits limits
In this mono-cultural world
That bids you keep consuming
And your banner tightly furled,
While all creations groaning
In a language still unborn —
If you would ever learn it
You must sink beneath the storm
Of this polluting culture
And its cruel dissecting knife —
Play your souls true instrument,
Join the symphony of life.

So why should I be preaching
Like some prophet sent from God?
I'm not — my heart is loaded
Like a 'brickie's' heavy hod.
It's laden with a challenge
Of reality so bright
I can't avoid the leading
Of this star within my night.
For I have seen the lovelight
Shining through my fathers eyes,
As stricken in his wheelchair
He prays, even as he dies
Dumbly with each heart — beat
His love — naked spirit leaps
Beyond his body's prison
To the world for which he weeps
Beyond his body's prison
His prayers reach through the bars —
For his transcendent spirit
Knows the dance — steps of the stars.

§

PRAYER TO MAMMON

Oh Mammon, Lord of England,
Begetter of our State,
Provider of our happiness,
Shaper of our fate:
Our families, our time and strength
We offer unto Thee;

To Thee we sacrifice our souls
And all our liberty.
We know who are thine enemies,
We know them very well,
And we'll ensure they bend the knee,
And worship thee in Hell.

It's the jobless and the scrounger
The gay, the homeless poor,
The traveller, the squatter,
The immigrant, the whore.

It's the Germans and the Spanish,
The French and Japanese,
The Jews, the Argentineans,
The Irish and Chinese.

It's Socialists and Liberals,
And Euro-Bureaucrats,
Social Workers and *do-gooders*,
And lefty *Guardian* hacks.

Send a strong, dynamic Leader
To cleanse our idle State
Of foreigners and dissidents,
And make our country 'Great'.

§

THE SLAVE'S PRAYER

Our Mammon who rules the Earth,
Hallowed be your Lottery.
Your kingdom come, your will be done
By governments as it is on the free market.
Give us this day our daily profit,
And chastise the poor and lazy
As we chastise ourselves,
And deliver us from inflation.
For your's is the kingdom
The power and the glory,
For hell and forever.

Amen

§

HOLIDAY

Sea-washed, light-stroked souls
Supine on towel-shares of shore line
Being baptised of toxic care
By the smiling sun.

Wash away worries
In the wound-free wandering waves
They never reach the beach again
Pock-mark your soul-tan.

There's a TV shore
Only a drive and switch away
It soaps the lounge of daily toil
By the mean moonlight.

WAKENING ANGER

Pour the petrol of freedom
Onto the flame of the Spirit.
Make a conflagration of the petty-minded.
If reality confuses them —
Blind them with it.

Nature writhes
The Planet dies
Let them expire
Cursing a God they don't believe in
Crucified on crosses of safety.
Why use persuasion or reason
On those who divorce reason from fellow-feeling
Who curse the surging tide
From the walls of their sandcastles.
When, eventually,
They have built the strongest microscope
To analyse their predicament
They will gaze at the fragments of their souls
And weep bitter tears over the ruined planet

§

WORDS, FIRE, WATER

Words I no longer expect you to understand
Yearning for communication
You hide in a desert of words
Measuring them out in metered stabs
Your call is too small for me
I want to live.

Fire You would rather die slowly
Recording — endlessly recording your actions
To the fire that is slowly consuming you.
You choke and cry as your prison fills
With the putrid stench of your fears
You believe light is the fire
It is — unless you abandon yourself to it.

Water In your poverty
You construct daydreams of clouds.
Who will remember yours?
Will they recognise them over the next horizon?
Will the people of tomorrow look up
And, seeing, sing the song you sang
With thankfulness and joy?
The clouds are beginning to boil
The light is breaking through
Every mental construct
And petty rationalisation
There can be no hiding now

The Lotus opens
The Kingdom comes.

ADVENT

From the quantum of the spirit,
From the implicate unbound,
Bursting the death-barred gates to peace
Leaps the love of heaven's hound;
Cascading through each time-bound shore
In triumphant singing light
The echos of the ringing pean
Flood the vacuum of the night.
Divinity consumes the pain
Knitting Eden's cosmic break,
The time bound objectivity
Of the human schizoid's ache.

In the gentle nerve-soaked loving
So harmoniously wild,
Love's resonating symphony
Breathes through lion and through child.

§

CHRISTMAS

One clear, tax-pinching wintery night
Weeping with dung-trod tears,
Galaxies of anguished stars baptised
A baby with their prayers.
Rough sheperds, heaven-rinsed eyes assaulted,
Read the sky, left their sheep
To the whim of raiding wolf and bear
In answer to the deep

Hunger of the spirit, heart-shaped hope,
And found him there
Simply waiting — love's word embracing
Iron nails, wounds of fear.
The Wise Men knew the Spirit's breath could
Subvert the rule of gold,
The arrogance of frankincense and
Myrrh's life mocking mould.

And today, I wish it could be so,
And not some sweet mirage
Because if it were, I'd gladly shed
This tinselled camouflage,
And travel in hope each star — led night
To find the stable bare,
And 'mongst the straw, some wood and nails,
Yet feel him waiting there.

§

STERILE CRUCIFIXTION?

The age long cry of suffering
Of blooded beast and ravaged Earth's
No longer heard in Shopping Malls;
So what's a crucifixion worth?

The Founder died some time ago,
Didn't court the right investors
Lacked good PR and marketing
Plus experienced Directors.

It was a very good idea
It's what everybody wanted,
But a tortured image isn't fun
Today when we are bloated.

So ring the tills and cash the cheques
And stuff our bellies to the brim
Slobber each vicarious thrill
Inject ourselves with Coke and Gin.

Stuff the hindmost, stuff the cripple,
Stuff the poor, the weak and simple,
Stuff the hungry Third World farmer,
Stuff myself should I grow tearful.

When, in a glass or mirror clear,
I see a face — an empty bowl,
I'll pass it by without a glance
I will not recognise my soul.

§

EASTER QUESTIONS

If God upon a cross were hung,
And human flesh about him clung,
Nailed by the hammer hand of Mars,
Writhing beneath the weeping stars,
And cried into the galaxy—
'Speak— why have you abandoned me'?
I, too would echo his deep cry,
And weep beneath the empty sky;
For even I can sense such pain,
The nerve-seared limbs, the tortured brain;
Can feel a heart break and grow dumb,
No deeper, loving depths to plumb.
But where the sword from angry sky
To cleanse this bloody human stye?
If Justice here could be denied,
What hope for man or crucified?

Did he see down 2000 years,
Through bloody mists of human tears,
2000 years of genocide,
Of plunder, rape, infanticide,
Of wolves free-ranging 'mongst the sheep,
A harvest far too red to reap?

Your kingdom has not come on earth,
So what is this creation worth,
If resurrection is delayed
Till every innocent's betrayed.
Heaven and earth remain divorced,
And man still fears his holocaust.
Can it be only he who weeps,
While God his own dumb council keeps?

Faith lives alone, nuturing hope,
Religion sells surrealist soap
To cleanse, to ease the psychic pain,
A phantom light within the brain—
But where the Comforter's warm might
Between cold sheets without the light?
Yet hopful men still bend their knees
Before a billion calvarys,
Still wing their prayers upon a dove
To silence—that mute name for love.

Life's dissected 'neath man's scalpel
Watched by minaret and steeple,
A bastard vine grows in the shrine,
The nightmare of a Frankenstein,
The curse incarnate of man's birth
Is loosed upon the sons of earth.

Welcome, brave new revelation,
Genes evolve toward salvation,
Striving in the lumpen leaven,
Forming the new techno- heaven,
Where everything is quantified,
Tamed, costed and computerised,
And virtual man in virtual space
Is his own god by his own grace.

Emotionally, we hug the ground,
And wrap ourselves in light and sound,
But soar in intellectual flight
To understand the futherest light,
Plumb the quantum depths inside
The infinite from which we hide,
And grope in fear towards sweet love,
Shrouded within a tightening glove.

I know the carpenter was true
While asking God — but was it you?
For when this fragile earth was born,
A single raindrop in a storm,
The fall-out from that first Big Bang-
Did you form man with fear and fang?
Or was he conscious of your grace,
Your breath inside his garden-space?

If love was crucified that day,
There's nothing more that I can say
'Cept "It is finished", God AND Man—
But if there is some holy plan,
Some new Word from o'er the border
Of the implicate's strange order
To sound upon our time-bound shore,
And stream through every grieving pore,

Some balm to heal man's murderous mind,
A light that will not make him blind —
Before this earth's too wracked and dry,
Before the last white dove can't fly —
Speak — and if you've made loving vow
For Christ's sake deal your justice now,
If you still cry this earth to see,
If you who made the dark — made me.

§

EASTER AND US

So you rose — again?
Death we can understand;
A bloom fades, petalling the earth with scent,
And each of us, after composing
A choral of crying and laughter,
Losing and loving
Must leave our scratched recordings
In the libraries of the living
— and decompose
But rise again?
What is this music that we learn to sing
So haltingly,
Fumbling with the instruments
Of body and mind
In the nurturing ground of nature,
That grows into a conscious presence?

Like strings, we vibrate with sound,
Molecules and atoms
Resonating on the frequency of 3,
Begotten from the quantum
Of the everlasting,
Energetic now.

'In the beginning was the Word'

The conscious, creating sound
Weaving dimensions
Of time and space.
Is it so very hard to see
That our dimension of the 3,
This dynamic matter,
The very substance
Of each somatic weight —
A sun, a planet, an insect or a man
Dancing to an omnipresent wind
That gives to each a time and space
To listen and compose?
Music that resonates
Within a hell of 1
Or a heaven of 4 or 8?

'And the word became flesh'

The Dancing Lord comes through the door,
Pipes his universal song
To all the blind and crippled throng
That cower within their phantom walls.

'My kingdom is not from this dimension'

*'And from the third dimension
He rose again'.*

§

EASTER TODAY
(in appreciation of Sydney Carter)

You can blame it on the Synogogue
The Temple, Mosque or Church;
You can say they're bloody hypocrites
Just preaching from a perch;
You can dance around the ashara,
Play politics with bras,
Sit withdrawn in dust and ashes or
Seek guidance from the stars;
You can become a green ascetic
Knit woollies from a fleece
Give up women, drink and smoking and
Talk endlessly of peace;
Or you can give away your money,
A martyr to a cause,
Or attempt to be a humanist —
Make reasonable laws
For muggers, mobsters, masochists and
The cynical and mad,
Schizophrenics and sick paedophiles,
The clinically sad.
You can go to darkest Africa
And help the starving poor,
Or become a politician
Or some other social whore;
But whatever you deny yourself,
Where ere get your kicks
You'll hear the muffled oars approaching,
Glimpse Charon o'er the Styx,
That dark river of reality
That each moth — soul must pass,
Forsaken, alone and destitute—

It makes a bloody farce
Of all our plans and little daydreams,
Our petty loves and hates,
Fear of mockery, insurances,
The mortgage and the rates;
The rogue meteorite or earthquake
Or fatal accident,
Brain haemorrhage, cancerous tumour,
Food poisoning in Lent.

*"It's God they ought to crucify
instead of you and me,
I said to the carpenter
A hanging on the tree."*
(Sydney Carter)

§

EVENSONG

6-15pm — the single, tolling bell awakens,
Beating dully through the autumn gloaming,
Echoing in the souls of the faithful.
Muffle-coated, murmuring acknowledgement,
They gather to disperse around the nave,
Sinking stiffly, stoically
Onto habitual hassocks.
The boiler is off, and hungry chills
Creep freely round the rigid pews,
Nibbling the notices in the porch —
The Flower Rota, Archdeacon's visit
And the Cathedral Music Festival.
The candle bulbs in wrought iron rings
Glimmer in the polished brasses
And oak communion rail.
The remembered dead on marble plaques
Brood in the rafters, fanned by the prayers
Of those below; they only frown at change —
Electric light, the moving of the font.
The bellows of the organ rasp;
Knarled hands plough the worn octaves,
Releasing a comforting rotation of seasonal hymns.
A swish of surplice cassocks up the aisle
And stands to mediate the mystery.
The heart-beat of the spirit,
Embedded in the natural round —
Unheard, ignored by maddened, market driven men —
Begins to pulse — massaged by the liturgy
And the still, small communion of the living saints,
Whispering softly of the love that overcomes.

Part 3:
People and Politics

FATHER

He lies like a beached whale
On the shore of eternity
Listening to the singing ocean,
Lapped by its waves,
The freeing tide
That will soon embrace him,
Teach him to dance again.
When I come in, his eyes gleam
And water. Dumb for twelve years,
He grips my hand
With his only moving limb,
Draws me down to kiss my cheek
Like a child;
So strong, so forthright in mind.
I am six years old again
Seeing that same hand grip a spade —
Monday — blessed Monday — his one day off.
The smell of his leather-patched tweed jacket,
His talisman of freedom
From the tensions of a city parish.
The damned energies brake,
Flowing down the handle
Turning the soil
Bending, pulling out the strands of couch,
Redeeming the ground,
Planting the good seed.
The terrier and I watch:
Eventually, he straightens — smiles
Leads me to my own small patch
By the clumps of Golden Rod
To plant some nasturtiums.

At least eight parishes have felt
His nurturing hand.
Abandoned by the disincarnate,
Whose words never take root
In heart or soil,
His living faith grew
Fruit, flowers and vegetables,
Husbanded chickens, goats and horses
And comforted the sick and grieving.
The balmy scent of Eden blew
Through the battlefield of his heart,
And the alchemy of love
Transmuted fear to faith.
But now, he can only watch
And listen to his only love
Drifting in and out of dementia
- But still attending, touching, kissing.
Yes — this will remain

Always

Eternal.

§

MOTHER

I knew an orphaned mother,
As vulnerable and dependent
As a stray lamb
On a snow-bound moor that's
Brought within a winter fold
Of fatalistic ewes
Bleating their "don'ts" and "oughts",
The authoritarian echoes
Of strict, religious shepherds.
"One day, the Good Shepherd will come,
Take you from these dying pastures,
Lead you beside the still waters of comfort —
But not now — and only if you're good.
So tighten your corset,
Feel the sharp herringbone fears
That will make your body bleed with guilt;
Abase yourself, so that being unnoticed,
You may more freely serve the righteous."
In the Spring of her life
She had no father's hand to hold,
No father's voice to praise,
To adore her aching, opening flower:
But, she had her poetry,
The doomed heroes of the First World War,
The wanderer's songs of the Sussex Downs
Echoing the joys of happier, simple days
Exquisite rural pictures that only focus
When the starving War Dragon
Demands blood and recompense,
And the cream of young, brave knights
Prepare to ride out again
To give battle.

Shades of doomed fatherhoods.
And then he, who'd missed the last battle,
That war to end all wars,
Took her riding over the Downs
And haltingly, sang his own poetic songs,
Deepening melodes that spoke
Of his desire to find the Grail
And she—she was content to adore
And help him in his spiritual quest.
Down sixty long, labyrinthine years
She worshipped him as God,
As he—as physical as Adam
Strove to reawaken Eden.
But now — now the lost father
Has returned to haunt her;
The fretful worship is not enough,
She must face the primal loss,
The repressed fears and pain
That bubble up like a demented spring
Dribbling suspicion over the banks
Of the sweet pool of reason;
And yet, knowing little now of time and place
She has unconcious knowledge
Of one eternal heart
Beating time with her's,
And, as the curtain tears
She will walk through hand in hand

With her lover

Her friend

Her father.

§

MOTHER LEAVING

Now the spirit, harshly breathing
Trembles in the wounded clay
Husband here, and first son calling
"Shall I go or shall I stay"

Beside her, bound within a wheelchair
He reaches out a stiffened hand
Caresses her unconscious fingers
Fondles her gold wedding band.

Does he see her green and tender
Riding o'er the Sussex Downs
In that long-ago September
Shining neath their lover's crowns.

I cry inside at this communion,
His yearning silence o'er her bed
Calming her staccato breathing
With Spirit wine and Spirit bread.

Dumb his lips and dumb his sorrow,
Numb his limbs and numb his pride
"I'll not need your urine bottle
I'll not leave my lover's side".

Now the evening shadows gather
Round the lovelight burning bright,
Clouds part — and for a moment
They are wreathed in shafts of light.

Immobile in the sterile side ward,
Transfixed by every drowning breath —
We hear it weaken — her final kisses
Blow towards us at her death.

Still their riding out together
Hand in hand towards death's gate
"I'll not leave you, I will follow,
You will not have long to wait."

§

CELEBRATING MOTHER

Having seen her off on her journey,
Now we gather to bury the bits
She leaves behind —
The particles of body and clothes
Drifting on the wave of her spirit,
And to celebrate the life
Resonating in our hearts and minds.
I push his wheelchair up,
Up the long bumpy hill of emotion
Into the church.
She has already preceded us;
Her oak coffin — like a family jewel box,
Garlanded with lilies
Trumpeting memories from their white mouths
Lies waiting in the naive.
In the front pew we sit down —
Staring — swallowing.
My brother grips my father's hand
In the wheelchair beside him
In the aisle.

So begins the celebration.
He, the dumb pilgrim, mouths the words
Nodding at their significance,
For this terminal liturgy
Speaks of Faith, Hope and Love,
And all of these are part of him
As they are of her.
I read from St John's Gospel
Of the raising of Lazarus —
But there is no movement
In that sacred box:
She is not here
In our struggling stream
Of time.
I read one of her favourite poems —
'In No Strange Land —
Inapprehensible, we touch thee',
And know — yes she is still with us
Walking along the bank
On the other side
With my brother
Looking over.
The priest — another brother
Announces a hymn.
(I wonder how many other brothers
could lead their own mothers funeral service)
'Thine be the glory — death has lost its sting'
In the sunlight, outside
I push the wheelchair up
Up to the top of the churchyard
Through the rigid guard of honour
Formed by the waiting dead,
He, clutching a red rose.

Against the far hedge,
A man lurks beneath a yew tree
Watching us silently process
Towards his yawning pit.
Prayers and birdsong.
As the boxed bits
Of wife, mother and friend
Are lowered slowly —
Finally —
From our sight,
The undertaker — tall, thin and gentle,
Casts a handful of topsoil
That patters down onto the jewel box
Like rice over a bride.
He can hardly reach
To cast his last red rose;
I push his wheelchair
Right up to the edge.
Finally, he flicks it over,
And we watch the blood — red
Tumble from sight
Into the dark.
It is finished.

I wheel him back.
He is not alone;
He has already let go
Of the bits,
And now, through the open eye
Of his heart
Feels her waiting
The end of his own long call of duty.
He is far more serene
Than I or my brothers.

§

CHILDREN

I am merely the unconscious springboard,
Kinetically untrained to your weight;
But yours is the perfect dive
I'd love to shoot — achingly
Downward me — upward you
Into perfect, symmetrical arcs,
Inspiring the vicarious crowds.
The springboard is buckled,
Cracked with my weaknesses,
Yet — faith, hope, love,
The greatest of these
Springs you forth
From the implicate order
Into the coming-now—
The shaping, self-determining
Unknown explicate
That resonates with echoes of
Shalom.

Do not grow weary
Dancing on the garbage
We have strewn
Across a mad millennial world.
Plunge your spirit deep within the earth
And help her
To bloom again.

§

SUICIDAL 'COMMUNICATION'

Did they say you never cried?
I still hear your hysterical songs,
Your frozen humour
Smooth and crystalline,
Deprecatingly laid down
For skating conversationalists
Scourging your hard back.

I have sensed the unfrozen
Submarine life
Autistically controlling the thaw;
Seen the drowning eye
Staring up at the light
Dancing dimly
Above its glass prison —
The manic activity,
Baby nails
Scraping and gouging
The coffin lid.

I cried too
As I tried to embrace your
Zero
Plunging my silly arms against the ice.
But then, you stopped struggling.
I watched —
Impotent
As you turned
And nose-dived
Into the mud.

LAST LETTER

Bardsey Island — alone
Rigid rock against desperate seas
A place of spirits
Bird — dreams circling
Prayer — calling
Winged unheard
From a mussled-soul
Alone

Birmingham — alone
Should I have responded
To the niggling peckings
In my breast?
But I was told you were
Away — physically
Not just in your mind
Even if I had
What difference, if you
Were still shut in — alone?

Were you always unborn,
Miming at the world
Umbilically bound to your rock,
An unhandled pearl
In a glass shell?
I remember — how I remember
The warmth of that shell,
Your generous, creative gestures.
Cannot even blood brothers
Ignorantly touch
The same rock
From which they were hewn?

Your last letter
I read sobbing
With Godfrey
In your room.
Yes — you were of sound mind
Yes — your faith in the power
Of eternal love
Overcame your fear
Of death's
Damaging legacy.

Appledore — alone.
This is only the second time
In seven years
I've read it.
So objective — so caring
So genuinely caring
Of everyone else.
You were a starving man
In the midst of caring people
Offering you food;
But your mussled heart
Could only filter
Emotional waste
Through its clammed shell.

So easy to open
If you swim
In self esteem;
But bound to your lonely rock
You still gave
Your last emotional mite
—And more
Without asking
For anything in return
Even love

And then in your last year
It did open a little
Once
She drew you out of your clammed heart —
But kissed too exquisitely
Your half grown pearl —
And you withdrew
Leaving her wondering
And you — self loathing
Locked up again
Alone

Perhaps if I had not
Cast away
Convention with its
Concrete 'oughts',
Thrown myself from my rock
into the ocean
I should have preceded
Your passing;
But I chose life
Clinging in desperate embrace
To a succession
Of swimming lovers
Until I learned
To live outside my shell
Touch and be touched

You taught me that
An ideal
Remains still-born,
Cannot be related to
—Or relate
Until opened in the waters.

Digested in the stomach
Of this world
It becomes food
For others and yourself;
Muddied and blooded
Emerges the individual
To make some sort of
Peace.

I tore it up,
I will not read it again,
Neither would I wish anyone else to;
But I have photos of you
And a typically detailed copy
Of your CV
(Yes, you did achieve so much)
So good-bye — for a while,
I am letting you go
I shall always miss you
Particularly when
I am alone
Revisiting
My own rock
Where we spent
Our growing years
Together

POSTSCRIPT

Self-Deception
After the devastation
The emotional earthquake
The burning
The tear-floods
The forged-forgetting
The manic reasoning—

slowly, we sought to re-colonise
the psychic slopes
of the crater
you left behind

But, last night
seven years later
without warning
explosion!
Molten anger burst
from my mouth
'You Bastard'
I raved
in my sleep
Pounding your spectre
in the air.
She told me about it
in the morning.
Yes, I've finally
Felt this too.

§

KINDNESS AND CRUELTY

Safe
Shell-bound
Comforting mother heat
Only an ego's beak
To break the tingling testa.

Pecking
Pierced membrane
Prison walls cracking
Cramped baby blood carousing
Relishing the fight for freedom.

Light
Urgent touch
Finger-tip ceasarian
Ego's beak weakening
Under a mother's death kiss

§

MYSELF

I have run my fingers around the intellectual shapes,
Picked them up, felt each persuasive weight,
The cerebral, light philosophies,
The heavier religions and ideologies —
All games conceived by nature's nurture;
Mystically experienced by one or two,
Intellectually formulated by the staid and respectable,
Historically filtered and adopted by traditionalists
To give meaning and continuity to kingdom or state.

I have wondered at the mystery of micro and macro,
The underlying illogicality of photonic beam/point,
Contemplated the paradox of illusion
And the anthropocentric lunacy
Of materialism and number
With its infinite, expanding maze of names
For each specialised, costed part.
I have smelt the wet earth
Clothed in her dawn's fresh musk,
Broadcasting her fecundity to the barren stars.
I have made love on that same earth,
Adam naked with my eager Eve
On a moor inside a Bronze Age circle
And felt primal ecstasy bursting through life's dream,
And felt no guilt or fear

But vulnerable and thankful for the grace.
I have drunk old wine slowly
And new — to excess — reliving bitter dregs —
A lonely youth, a rich old man,
And a beautiful, incurable woman:
The first threw himself from a cliff,
The second hung himself by his tie,
The third took an overdose.
I have seen my trusting children — eagerly learning,
Growing under encouragement, finding self-esteem
And becoming conciliatory towards their paternal misfit.
I have loved and danced and dared — yet
I will not sleep with pride —
The vanity of ambition in the face of death.
Above all, I cannot merely watch life pass
Vicariously viewing and listening
To spiritual and emotional illiterates,
Half-believers in everything,
Who take pride in praising cultural ephemera —
Artists mooning the stars,
Writers making a babel of meaning,
Frightened fundamentalists preaching faith,
Pontificating politicians;
Better the company and suspect honesty
Of whore and beggar
Or the singer groping for a song.

The earth groans under the weight of human stupidity;
The animals stare in disgust
And the birds shit on their palaces and temples —
I have become old too young.
I love enough to reach for hungry children's hands,
To give them bread and time
But the nervous herds of engorged adults

Poaching the earth in the broad gates
Of shopping malls and theme parks,
Draining the last water holes in the wilderness
Leave me cold and despairing.
Mystery and wonder — each dawn's revelation
Can bring no healing touch
To such a numbing, leprous culture
That chooses digitalisation
And virtual realities
In its vain effort to make the rampant earth
A global flim-set.
Only love remains,
Beating in the dark.
I will lean more heavily on this.

§

RE-ASSESMENT

I want to do
More than wait
Closeted in shrinking hours,
Carried around on the carousel
Watching the building and demolition,
The climate changes
In the faces of children,
And masked adults
Hoarding the spring
Pursued by mammon's
Time and motion
Meaninglessness.
I want to experience
Sacrament
In the frozen granite
Look up

And dance with the stars —
Burn with them
Burn the meteorites
Of pain, shame and
Small ignorant deaths.
Yes, more than just
A flickering candle,
Too small to read by
Too weak to warm.

§

HEDGE OR EDGE

Oh, I can grind uphill and down,
And throw my arms around the stars;
Still stare the depths of waiting graves,
Feel prisoned needs-embrace their bars;
Reach down the arms of love and hate
To play the games we prisoners play,
And drink the ticking time away.

Love's meaning is a waiting game
Of drab disguises, many names
Learned on metronomic journeys
Down dank canals, past rusting cranes.

No! Cast me crashing down the rocks,
Flash-flooding madly down the gorge
Of life's rich, hissing, shaping forge

—-before I reach that ox-bowed sleep,
Meandering through memory,
Grey-sleeping
To eternity.

DOORWAYS

Where is the room with two doors,
The Narnian wardrobe,
The entry to forever?
For here, in this compost of memory,
This towerblock of perceptions,
Every room in numbered,
The furtniture manufactured,
Intellectually arranged to individual taste —
But all the same,
No exit.

Away with virtual reality,
This miasma of veils.
Naked, I cross your threshold,
Enter your temple,
Sink through the dark warmth of your earth,
Down into the aquifer of the heart

Roots intertwined, our tendrils draw
The singing sap into the aching branches,
And nerve-leaves rustle
Through the silken canopy.

Lost in our lip-loving search,
The scent-savouring suckling,
Soul-warming, sweat simmering
Ballet of bodies
The cyclone breaks,
Buttocking us
Through the dissolving doorway of reason,
Roaring down through the curling white throat
On, on, on, on,

Into the limp warm shallows
Beside the oceans of dreams;
There, amid the lingering music,
The percussion of heartbeat,
The whisper-wind of breathing,
The stringed rain on the darkening window
We'll lie wombed from the world —
Until the cold moon drags back the tide
And the ruthless sun
Burns the shadows from the bare beach,
Re-casting us in gold
And I'll leave your white lodge
No exit.

§

THE GRAIL SEEKERS

As the sun spread her nectar
Of gold, rippling kisses
In a stream from her chalice
In a path to our feet,
The sea, drenched with summer
Tongued the sand — bid us follow
Down the jewelled highway
Westward and westward
Away from our shadows
To the end of the rainbow
Where the grail seekers meet.

Hand in hand we swam into
The featureless future
That encircles the present
And gnaws at the light —
Polar winds slashing

Smashing us southward
Down to the doldrums
Silent and listless
Lonely as phantoms
That drift through the night:
But we still held our course
To the grail of the West.

Then you faltered
And weakened
Could only tread water,
Fell asleep in my arms
Like a child on the breast
Till the eastern sky shaking
The peat from her shoulders
Lanced crimson towards us
Throwing off her disguise;
I told you I loved you
You wakened and murmured
Whispering my name
And smiled at the dawning
Beyond a night's mourning
Till the soul left your eyes.

So I handed you over
To the waiting wave-bearers
Who cradled and washed you
Keening with grief
As they carried you westward
And wrapped your sweet body,
Your pilgrim's brave body
In a white, spray-spun sheet.

I watched you slip downward
And cried for the white dove
Circling above me
Released to the skies
Singing its way homeward
Away to the westward
Calling me onward
Down the jewelled highway
Westward and westward
Away from my shadows
To the end of the rainbow
Where the grail seekers meet.

§

TELL THE SUN

Tell the sun I love her daughter,
Ripened neath her harvest moon
On a planet green with laughter,
On a perfumed meadow strewn
With velvet, blue and golden flowers
Bleeding colours through a dream
Throbbing with pellucid glory,
Lambent on a lyric stream.

Red-hued nipple buds are bursting,
Love-wine springs from out the earth—
Now the moment of creation,
Now the unnamed starts his birth.
Stay this timeless, oozing moment,
Cast it not upon the deep,
Where the separating shadows
Drag our souls back into sleep.

Let it fly—the wanton wind that
Gales herself through every tree-
Winters our waiting—-composing-
A new, eternal symphony.

Tell the sun I love her daughter,
Licked her aching, salty sea
Felt her swallow all my longing,
Felt her give herself to me.

§

L

High upon the slopes of Cawsand
She springs the purple heather,
Running free as the wild west wind
On wings of moorland weather.

Across to grey-stacked Hangingstone,
Rhythmic in her easy pace
The skylark lifts her soul to share
The communion of its space.

Still those lithe, tanned legs are flying
Past a blackthorn streamed with wool,
Leaping over peat-brown brooklets
Driving on to Cranmere Pool

There she stops and looks about her,
Lycra slips from breasts and thighs
Woman in the dappled waters,
Eve beneath the smiling skies.

Stands and cups the cooling liquid
Throws it in the sparkling air
Silver streams of licking wetness
Livens hunger for me there.

Now the rock of Kestor calls her
In the mewling, raptor's shriek
Celtic princess, bronzed as moorland
Stands atop her kingdom's peak.

Scorhill's magic circle sees her
Wreath-like in the kissing mist
Torques of silver round her ankles
Silver bracelets on her wrist.

Guardian riders form above her
Lone upon the shadowed moor
Baptise her with a cooling sky-spring
Race her up to Shilstone Tor.

On by Shilly Pool to Cawsand,
Stone lines mark a funerary way
Stops — and sees again the passing
Echoed pictures of that day.

Sees a bronze and iron army
Bravely march towards the hill
Sees it open, sees it swallow
Feels their waiting, feels their chill.

Salutes, and turns — bounding forward
Through the white-topped cotton grass
Red-robed fox in wind-bowed oak clump
Calls a greeting, scents her pass.

STRANGER

Still I see her in Skaig valley
Running up to Belstone Tor
Laughing in the life around her
Woman on the darkning moor.

§

YOU AND I

When I was in Australia,
Mind and body surfing
Through Poseidon and philosophy,
A brash bush-baby
In fishing boat and mining town
In a hard, tanned skin,
You were in London
At the fag-end of the sixties,
An Appledore maid
With long, blond hair
Cascading down your Afghan,
Looking for the main-line,
The fresh and easy freedom
Of devil may care.

Twenty years later,
Heart-shells split open,
Precious pearls exposed,
Two bar stools waited,
The needy blood flowed
Dissolving differences
In a mad, aching alchemy —
Wilder for its wanting,
More urgent than the moment,
Sweeter than a strawberry,
Softer than a cloud.

But you cannot sprint a marathon,
You cannot spring the years,
After harvest comes the sowing
The watering with tears.
Our hearts sank through the waters,
The belonging stranger's pain
Beside a family funeral plot,
Protected from the rain

The bar stools now are vacant,
But when we meet upon a beach
We know the pearls within the oyster
Are touched, but out of reach.

§

SIREN

Oh tempt me not with this illusive dream,
The tresses of your lustrous hair
The nippled bosoms, eager — bare
The bushy lips so hungry spread
This siren softly makes me dread
All others that I've felt and seen.

Shall I choose drowning ? Tempt me not with death.
I'll meet you on my temple's mount
Or not at all; for I can count
The empty forms to me I drew
Spiritless — I would know you through
And feel your scented, aching breath.

§

THE GOODBYE MAN

An armchair and a thin, grey man:
A universe of spectral dreams;
He fought the battles of his time
And now sits musing in the streams
Of love and hate and hope and fear,
Of now and when and why and how —
He does not criticise so much
But contemplates the newsprint now —
The weave, the warp, the hidden side,
His life within the maze of thread;
He looks back from the mountain top,
I see that look — and softly tread
On past him to an empty chair,
Take up my paper — spread my wings
Around the world — the page is bare,
Drum — empty of enduring things !
I glance across — he knows I see
And smiles a last goodbye to me.

§

ON THE BREAKING OF GODS

2000 Years since
The King of Hearts was crucified —
Long live the Queen of Hearts,
Rocketed to the heavens,
Fragile beacon,
Glamorous dream-star
Yet incarnate — media manufactured,
Our own human satelite —
Explodes — before her time —
A feeding-frenzy at the last communion,
Gobbling the fragrant fragments
Before they disappear
Into the black hole.

In such a vacuous world,
Privacies, intimacies quantified,
Analysed away,
Princes still grieve,
Prodded by the nervless stumps
Of leprous media kings.

What god shall we create next —
In our own image?
A King of Diamonds — a mega — mogul?
A King of Spades — a dark angel?
How shall we worship?
How shall we kill it?

§

DIANA

Dream-star hunting in the skies,
Crashes through the media net;
Dumb the Queen of staring eyes
Beyond the royal sunset.

Glamorous hopes were fashioned
And rocketed into space,
Beautiful, fragile capsule-
Aphrodite's human face,

That revealed to each an aspect
Of their uncompleted chart,
The Shangri-La of innocence,
The mute language of the heart.

§

SIR RUPERT MUDSUCK-GUTTERPEER

Sir Rupert Mudsuck-Gutterpeer
Had a solid sterling heart,
A thorough dollar-driven mind
That could tear a man apart,
And price his personality,
His clothes, his dreams, his loyalty,
And then buy him like a tart.

He bought and sold MPs like slaves
To build his media empire;
He raised them up and cut them down,
Then selected more to hire:
This buccaneer of industry
Controlled all their publicity
Chose the music for their choir.

Sir Rupert—most concerned for
The morals of the nation,
'Correctness' and conformity
Produce a neat equation—
Job-safety and servility =
Increasing productivity
Which helps reduce inflation.

So every day there thundered forth
From out his tabloid papers
Sour diatribes against the poor,
The Welfare State and scroungers;
But then he always sweetened it
With fresh sprinklings of bum and tit—
Plain diets need their peppers!

Sir Rupert's empire spanned the world,
He owned papers, film, T.V.
'Till every human's thoughts were shaped
By this mogul's industry;
But yesterday — nobody cried,
For yesterday Sir Rupert died
Sitting on his lavatory.

Oblivious of the heavenly light,
Unaware that he had died,
He rudely banged the golden door,
Filled with grandeur, puffed with pride,
Demanding entry straight away—
'So how much is it? I can pay'.
Peter looked at him and sighed,
'Your credit is quite worthless here,
Sir Rupert Mudsuck-Gutterpeer'.

LOSERS AND LOVERS

Metro-man in the middle lane
With tabloid mind and A4 brain.
Still-born, snail-safe statistician,
Life's deadening drone
Predictable, derisable,
Respectable, forgetable,
Bureaucratic clone:
Sighs a last petition,
Loves alone.

Desperate artist sucks life's tit,
Hungrily drains each drop of it;
Drunken, spawns a new creation,
Life's poor weeping wit,
So ostentatiously conscious,
So dangerously contagious,
Memorable shit
Final shout of freedom,
Life's love lit.

§

TIME SERVER

I sacrificed my childhood dreams,
Worshiped those I did not own,
Reflected other people's thoughts,
Loyal ape behind the throne.

Carefully oiling all who led
And my fail-safe pension plan,
I safely climbed each greasy rung
As the trusted 'info-man'.

And now I'm happily retired,
A Rotarian true and blue,
I think I'll give some time to God
And try his insurance too.

§

ROTARY WATCH

I, with fire in my belly,
Watch you every Thursday
Sipping your pre-Rotary drink
Waiting — as you have always waited
For your life to begin,
Dressed in pressed grey
For safety.
You have read the *Daily Express*
And now await your fellows
To vent your spite on questioners
And non-conformists.
Thank you for fighting in the war
Were you a clerk?
Or did you storm the beaches
And now wonder why?
After all, the Germans are now our friends
And own Rover.
I am sorry to expect more of you
It's just that I can't stand waste
And studied indifference.
I wish you would break out of the straight-jacket
Of your solid reputation
Now while the ambient music plays
Born Free.

SELF — MADE

You've got the house
The suit, the cars
And pretty wife Virginia
Three kids away at Private Schools
A beach house in Madeira
Maturing PEPS
Insurances
And your Private Health Care Plan,
Green wellies, Barbour, Labrador
And a flat above for Gran —
But can you hear
A robin weep
See the poisoned petal fall
Smell children on a rubbish heap
Where they scavenge in Bengal?
Is your laughter
Just an echo
In the chasm of the night,
A hard cocktail for the moment
To help blind you to the light?

§

ABUSED

Take off your armour
Let me see
The tender, pining, red — raw god,
The heart — blood of integrity,
The virgin in its
Blighted pod —
The filthy failure
Soiled in youth
By brutal — soft marauding hands
That fondled trust — then shattered truth
And threw it on the
Wilting sands.
But yours is not a
Barren shoot
Malformed within a soiled bed,
This cleansing shower shall wake the fruit
If you but lift your
Prickly head.

§

EVIL SPERM

'Late, late at night you came to me
Huge bearded man all cloaked in red'.
"Take off your nightdress little girl
I'll place a stocking by your bed.

Tell not your mother or a priest,
For you are but a child of hell
Horned demons in the cellar wait
Inprisoned in your inner well—

Whose depths I know are sacrosanct
As virgin as my tiny bum
My father penetrated deep
And left an ache I cannot plumb."

'My father's hands had steel claws
That played me like a captured mouse,
The shame, the shame — the bitter shame
A girl — boy thing, a ransacked house.

Your poisoned, putrefying sperm,
Injected like a stinging bee
Has made trust septic in my heart,
And every man untrustworthy.

Jesus, my God I am your child,
Forbid me not to come to thee
Through your strong man all cloaked in black,
The shepherd of your family.

In mad confusion, choked with tears
I made confession to my priest'
"Take of your panties goddess-girl,
Relieve the hunger of this beast.

Tell not your mother or a friend
For you are but a child of hell,
Horned demons in the cellar wait
To torture you if you should tell."

'How can I touch or look full face
Hungering for a man's true love
Expecting that I'll be berayed,
Quicksand within — wild faith above.'

Hang thirteen millstones round his neck
And throw him in the deepest sea
The man who's lust berayed us all
Who's seed is death to life in me.'

§

GUNS

'I sold four guns in sweet Dunblane
To a lonely man with an angry brain.
I knew him well, he kept the law
'For sport' he said, and I closed my door.

I sold guns to Saddam Hussein
A lonely man with an angry brain.
I knew him well, he was at war
'For peace' he said, and I closed my door.

Sixteen infants — the man's insane!
I knew every one; I'm not to blame.
Laid my wreath on the red gym floor,
Wrung my hands, and then closed my door.

Guns secure jobs, and foreign pain
Is not like it is in sweet Dunblane.
Gun exports are approved by law,
'Cause five thousand Kurds don't live next door'

§

FOR THE LOVE OF IRELAND

Does Jesus live with Loyalists
Constructing ethnic walls?
Does Jesus live with Nationalists
A-plotting in the Falls?

Does Jesus need an army to
Defend his 'godly' state,
Need pipes and drums and Orangemen
To bomb and march and hate?

Does Jesus need an army to
Unite the Irish State,
Need cells of Green Republicans
To bomb and shoot and hate?

Jesus lives in Ulster and wears
A Green and Orange sash;
His back is soaked in crimson from
The Green and Orange lash.

See — the noblest blood flows deepest
Where pride and fear have bled.
Hear — the Kings of Tara calling
A Brotherhood of Red.

§

IN THE MAZE

H—Block
[H-eternal paralells with a hyphen in between:
Block-a dead end]

In the Maze,
Immured inside
For Ireland's glory,
Ulster's pride.

—cause my heart is mined,
My mind is rabid,
Beyond the razor-wire
Homeless, nomadic;
A jackal in the bitter night
Circling the human camp-fires.

One Catholic for a Prot,
Christ—why not?
It's my small world that matters,
My unmade life in tatters.
I blame your pain—
Which is not as deep as mine,
And God-you're not as hard.
I'm not crucified for me—
No-but that others can be free
– – – Of you.
My lonely deprivation
Is your fucking sick invention
– – – I'm free!
If a martyr I should die,
Or I hear your last screamed cry
As we drive you from our Eden

While the pipes are sounding Freedom-
By Christ we'll have a rave
As we stamp upon your grave!
Global Markets — Global Warming?
I'll damn you to the morning,
And chase you down to hell,
Ay, and the Eurocrats as well
– – – Cause fears become my meaning,
And my faith—eternal dreaming.

Was I ever once alive,
Or do I just survive?

§

'THE STATE WE'RE IN'

tradition

Our historical traditions,
The ritual pageantry
Of Law and Church and Parliament
Soap-opera monarchy,
Give citizens a sense of worth
And bind them to the State,
Protest can then be shown to be
Disloyalty or hate.

government

Industrialists pay the Party
And organise the Press.
The Party appoints the Quangos;
And untoward excess
Of minority opinion
Not orthodox or 'straights'
Firmly under the dominion
Of MI5's Estate.

While the Councillors sit begging
Outside the Treasury door
For handouts from a Ministry
To house the restless poor,
Rich Ministers in Limousines
Protected to the last
By Directorships and 'kickbacks'
Sweep regally on past.

welfare state
The Oligarchy's now agreed
Society's a-gonner
Each individual must be left
Fighting their own corner
And those who laboured, paid their dues
Into the welfare state,
Must reinsure if they want 'care'
After their sell-by date.

Now, responsible, wise virgins
Sign Private Health Care Plans
So they never have to worry;
They'll get the best bedpans.
But scrounging, unwise virgins
Who do not plan ahead
Will have to wait at least two years
Before they get a bed.

youth
Angry, youthful hearts are crying
For bread instead of stones,
And sharp, youthful teeth are tearing
The flesh from off the bones
Of the powerful, monied classes
Whose rotting, law-sharp tooth
Bites back—and grimly contemplates
The anarchy of youth.

countryside

The 'Sceptred Isle' lies weeping,
Road-scarred and quarried deep.
Through her moors and fields and rivers
The poisons slowly creep.
Fenced wilderness is quantified
And the wildlife's dethroned
Communion's a mere lollipop
Now bird and beast are owned.

heritage

There is the National Heritage
The sentimental dream
Of warm beer by the pub log fire
And cricket on the green,
And Interpretation Centres
To tell what we have lost,
And of what our parents fought for
And just how much it cost.

church

Nice, respectable Church people
Debate their liturgy
And whether women should be Priests,
Things revolutionary!
If Jesus was as nice as them
His voice might still be heard,
But then, he didn't have to stand
Twixt Mammon and The Word.

god?

Production is the national god,
There's no alternative.
We must compete, we must prevail,
We, above all, must live.
If whiskey, cars and armaments
Are what we're good at making,
We'll force the poor to buy from us,
'Fleece' them in the taking.

vision

But underneath this thistle park
Of overshadowing weeds
Albion's old soil is being stirred
By new and precious seeds
Of green visions, bright and global
But local in their deed
And a raw determination
To see them all succeed.

As the grass roots army marches
The International Drum's
Being heard by Wing Commanders
And the poets of the Somme
And the brave and gentle Dongas
And those at Brightlingsea
And each spectral non-conformist
Of Albion's history

And the markets will be shaken
By this gathering storm
As the little people waken
And springing hope is born.
Then animals will lift their heads
And birds renew their song
Each life will know each other
And each to each belong.

IN ENGLAND NOW

England's become very elderly,
Even the young men are grey
Programmers, consultants, accountants
Costing the value of play

Art is a modernist's Tate-dream
Feted by posers and cranks,
A cynical boast of disgorgement
Rated by boardrooms and banks

Religion is sexual repression,
Moral crusade on the psyche
Conforming, dividing, conforming,
Loving itself on a knife

Politicians — mercenary weasels,
The morally lacquered bore
Who's sure the old nag in the stable's
The one that died in the war

Farmers are now techno-managers —
Stock genetically planned, and
Corn that's been chemically pissed on —
Raped is the flower of the land

Bid adieu to communication
To the songs of love and birth;
Information hails from souless skies
On the eyeless men of earth

§

THE LOST MILLENIUM

In the wilderness they'd listened
To the ranting Grantham witch,
'The earth shall be inherited
By the scheming and the rich'.
New Labour's prophets marvelled at
This universal law,
The First and Great Commandment
Long locked within the Testament
The Good News for the poor.

So forward to the new Millenium,
To the shining Blair-built Dome,
The techno-New Jerusalem
That calls every Briton home.
Join the statutory pilgrimage,
Let's restore our national pride,
The New Market Forces Gospel
Shall be our spiritual guide.
So goad them, beat them, tax them,
We'll only relax when
Every Briton is a clone.

In the wilderness they're searching
For a single Tory track,
While those in the van cry 'sceptic',
And those to the fore cry 'back'.
See how transcendent is their worship
Of their tarnished Golden Calf,
As their Guru flies and hovers,
'Om' — chanting as he wavers
Over each embittered half.

Forward to the New Millenium
With someone vaguely Hague, a
Bald embryo of everyman,
Grey-suited, sober grave;
With his elderly supporters
And embittered sceptic band,
He'll lead the nation's exodus
From the hated Euro-Land.
So seduce them, grease them, woo them,
We'll only relax when
Every Tory is a drone.

§

THE OLD STORY

Said the serpent to the lady,
Softly hissing — belly flat,
'Dreamy Adam will not love you
If your stomach turns to fat;
If your empty breasts sag heavy
And you grow a double chin—
Take this apple, and keep yourself
Firm, voluptuous and trim.'
Said the liberated lady
To the snake upon the bough,
'I really couldn't give a fig,
I've a lesbian lover now;
Adam is so pre-occupied
Watching Able play with Cane
With a prehistoric football—
And he says that I'm to blame!
He was such a caring lover —
Up to when the kids were born
We romped naked in the forest,
And made endless love till dawn.'
But the snake replied 'You're lying,
You are lying through your teeth,
There's not another lady yet;
Though he never wears a sheath
You still haven't had a daughter,
And there are no shopping malls
For a girls' day out together,
A poor substitute for balls;
But just wait a few millenia
You'll have lovers, malls and balls,
In the meantime, take this medicine,
Take this apple 'ere it falls,'

SONG

MOVE ON

Move on, climb your mountain
Move on, find your dream
We'll meet again some new morning
Tell each other what we've seen

Move on, your bud must open
Feel the wind, the frost and rain
Move on, your life is waiting
Move on, and find your Name

Move on, don't look behind you
Move on, don't feel ashamed
You can stand upon my shoulders
I never want to see you tamed.

Move on, find your own meaning
You can't live within my shade
Move on, new friends are waiting
Move on, don't be afraid.

(REPEAT FIRST VERSE)

Jeremy Bell
5/1/99